Goodbye, Hello!

Written by
Rob Waring and **Maurice Jamall**

HEINLE
CENGAGE Learning

Australia • Brazil • Japan • Korea • Mexico • Singapore • Spain • United Kingdom • United States

Before You Read

to fall

birthday

brother

car

cart

class

shopping

sister

smile

snowboard

store

beautiful

little

big

sad

the OLIVIERAS

HAPPY BIRTHDAY TO YOU!!

the OLIVIERAS

In the story

Alex

Daniela

Jessica

Jenny

"Come on, Daniela. Let's go in here," says Alex.
Daniela and her brother Alex are shopping.
It is their mother's birthday on Thursday.
Alex and Daniela go into a big store.

Daniela looks at the CDs. "Look! It's here!" she says.
"What's here?" asks Alex.
Daniela says, "It's the CD by The Bandits."
"Oh, really?" says Alex, but he is not looking.

Alex is looking at the snowboards.
"Wow," he thinks. "I want *this* for my birthday!"
"Daniela, look at this," he says.
Daniela does not look. She is walking away.
A little girl is coming with a shopping cart.

The little girl is not looking. She does not see Alex.
"Look out!" says a man.
The girl hits Alex with the shopping cart.
"*Ouch!*" says Alex. He falls into the snowboards.

The snowboards fall onto Alex. "*Ouch*!" he says.
"Hey! What are you doing?"
He is very angry with the little girl.
The little girl says, "I'm sorry. Are you okay?"
"No, I'm not," he says.

A girl in red comes to them.
"Are you okay, Jessica?" she asks the little girl.
Jessica says, "I'm okay."
"Say sorry to the boy, Jessica!" says the girl.
"I'm sorry," says Jessica.
Alex looks at the girl in red. He thinks, "Wow!
She's very beautiful!"

"I'm sorry," says the beautiful girl. "Are . . . are you okay?"
Alex says, "Umm . . . Umm . . . I'm okay. I'm really okay,
thank you. Thank you!"
She looks at Alex. Alex looks at her. They smile.

The girl in red goes away.
"Goodbye," she says. She smiles
at Alex.
Alex looks at the girl. "Yeah,"
says Alex. "Bye."
He thinks, "I want to talk to her."
Alex looks at her. He thinks she is
very beautiful.
He thinks, "What's her name?"

Alex sees Daniela. "Daniela, what's that girl's name?" he asks.
"I don't know," she says. "Why?"
Alex says, "Oh, okay. Bye!"
"What? Alex! Where are you going?" she asks.
"Bye," he says. "I'm going now."
"But Alex . . . these bags . . . ," she says. "Don't go away!"
Alex does not listen. He wants to talk to the girl.

Alex goes out of the store. He sees the girl.
He thinks, "She's very beautiful. She's smiling at me."
Alex wants to talk to her.
"What's her name?" he thinks. "I like her, but does she like me?"
"I want to talk to her. I want to know her name," he thinks.

The girl's mother comes. Jessica gets into the car.
"Oh, no!" he thinks. "I don't know her name!"
"Oh no! She's going . . . ," he thinks. "She's going!"
The girl in red gets into the car.

Alex is sad, but the girl is smiling at him from the car.
The car goes away and Alex looks at her.
"She likes me!" he thinks. "But she's going! Oh no!"
He is happy, but he is sad.

Alex is in class. He is sad. He is thinking about the girl.
He wants to see her.
"Okay, everybody," says Mr. Williams. "Please listen."
But Alex does not listen to Mr. Williams.

"We have a new student today. This is Jenny Martin,"
says Mr. Williams.
Alex thinks, "It's the girl in red! She's in my class!"
The girl sees Alex and she comes to him.
She says, "Do you remember me?"
"Yes. And I remember your sister," he says smiling.
"Hello, I'm Alex."
She smiles and says, "I'm Jenny. Hello!"